THE
SUGAR ORCHARD

Linda Diane Lay

Angelia Richhart, Amber Richhart

The Lay Family

Books
By

Poetic Colors

The Essence of a Pearl

Divinely Guided: Faith, Love, Hope, Peace & Joy

THE SUGAR ORCHARD

Written by:

Linda Diane Lay,

Angelia Richhart, Amber Richhart

Lay Family Publishing

Title: The Sugar Orchard

Copyright ©2016 Lay Family Publishing
Authors: Linda Diane Lay, Angelia Richhart, Amber Richhart, Lay Family &
The Royal House of Normandy Royal Lay Family

Tittle: The Sugar Orchard
Authors: Linda Diane Lay, Amber Richhart, Angelia Richhart, Lay Family &
The Royal House of Normandy Royal Lay Family
Description: Volume of free verse poetry
Identifiers:
(Paperback ISBN:978-1-300-21243-0) (Paperback ISBN: 9798224185238)
(E-book ISBN: 9798201433857) (Hardcover ISBN: 978-1-300-48050-1)

Subjects: Classification BISAC (North America)
POE024000   POETRY / Women Authors
POE001000   POETRY / Anthologies (Multiple Authors)
POE005010   POETRY / American / General
POE023030   POETRY / Subjects & Themes / Animals & Nature

Lay Family Publishing - Published & Printed in the
United States of America

10   9   8   7   6   5   4   3   2   1

Lay Family Publishing

TABLE OF CONTENTS

LOVE LETTERS

FREE GIFT

She always looked for something more than this world
could give.

Never standing in secrecy,

as she knew this wasn't how to live.

With her dreams and aspirations always tucked away in
her heart,

she always seemed to gleam even though this world
tried to tear her apart.

She always kept her faith,

for she knew in it she was strong.

But never understanding the world and all the things
that were wrong.

She never gave up hope when things seemed dark and
bleak,

but she did give up her life to Christ and became

truly free.

A Starry Night

As romance fills the air on a warm and starry night,

I found my love sitting amongst the candles-forbidden light.

Sitting so patiently,

waiting for me to diligently arrive.

As I walked up to him,

we gazed into each other's soulful eyes.

as I had missed him much,

as this was no surprise.

I sat with him till morning until the sun began to rise.

As my heart yearned to be with him,

I never wanted to say goodbye.

My heart began to crumble as we had to go our separate ways,

but this love I'll remember in so many beautiful ways.

A Morning Kiss

He always kissed my forehead,

every morning I awoke.

Letting me know I was cherished,

even though we never spoke.

Sentimental gestures are what he always chose,

as our heartfelt desires were always being very close.

CIRCLE OF LOVE

For she believed love was like a circle,

that never truly ended.

That love was a harbinger of many precious gifts,

if we were to love like God intended.

DIVINELY GUIDED

She always believed in fate not knowing what it would bring,

but knowing God was never late made her heart always sing.

For she knew he was always there every step of the way,

leading and guiding her in his divinely guided ways.

\

TRUE LOVES TEST

She loved the idea of love and all that it entailed,
she even loved the old stories of love like the unforgotten
fairy tales.

Not because they were perfect and not because they were
real,

but because they represented a love that never seemed to
fail.

She never believed love was perfect,

but she did believe love was true.

She believed true love was accepting each other's faults
and always being there for you.

Through life's beautiful journeys and the trials that come
with time,

she believed true love was strong enough to last the test
of time.

BLOSSOMS OF LOVE

Your lips touched mine and I instantly knew,

I would never want anyone else in my life but you.

You stained my heart like a watermark,

that could never be removed.

My heart became full of love,

as though a flower blooms.

I knew this love ran deep,

as you made me feel whole.

The love you gave me to keep,

filled my very soul.

LOVE OF GOD

For she always treasured love and all that it could give,
it could even replenish a souls will to truly live.

For love covers a multitude of sins we always bear,

the beautiful thing about love is that it neither judges
nor does it care.

It never cares about our mistakes, our imperfections,

or our flaws.

Love is always there to catch us when we happen to fall.

Love is truly beautiful,

and I hope you get to see,

the way God intended love to always be.

LOVING MEMORIES

Your eyes were as beautiful as the bright blue day,

I never underestimated the love in your gaze.

The moment I met you I felt overwhelmingly weak,

as my heart seemed to flutter and skip a beat.

I was always lost for words as you knew exactly what to say,

these are some of the memories that I will always replay.

From heartfelt moments to a lover's embrace,

these are the things that I would never change.

BEAUTY IN LIFE

A loving and faithful heart is the world's rarest gift,
for finding true love that will last a lifetime is a blissful
and beautiful gift.

For things here in this world never seem to last too long,

but is it because we are too scared to jump the cliff to
find an undying love?

For most of us usually just go with the course of life,

hoping one day we will find the beauty that lies in life.

Always hoping and always wondering how,

giving in to destiny and watching fate work it out.

THE MOONLIGHT'S RAYS

When we dream of love and life,
in the midst of our days.

We reminisce about the sweetest moments in the
moonlight's rays.

Hearing the somber sounds of crickets at play,

and knowing the sweetness and the nectar of life is in
our divinely guided ways.

I can hear the ocean tides roar into waves,

roaring in the night in the moonlight's rays.

As I stand on the shore,

I can see the boats docked in the bays.

As I began to walk to the pier in the moonlight's rays.

Always feeling led to the ocean is the calling of my life,

because for me it holds all the sweetness and the
nectar of life.

THE OLD OAK TREE

Life is so beautiful and yet so free,

when I dream and reminisce under the old oak tree.

As I grip the chains upon thy swing and press back and lean
in to begin to swing,

I remember all the moments I once have had.

With all the laughter and joy,

my heart was glad.

I look at today and where I am,

understanding life, love and the simplicity of man.

TRUE BEAUTY

Her love was beautiful and yet so true,

that many adored her love like a precious virtue.

For her beauty was rare like that of a precious stone,

and her heart spoke with care with every word that she

spoke.

THE BALLROOM FLOOR

I hear the symphony of a lovely

love song,

as the piano keys slowly played along.

In life and love we danced till light,

hoping love would soon

take flight.

He led the way onto the ballroom floor,

as my gown swayed back and forth in the midnight lore.

The lights were dim,

but I could feel his touch.

As we danced till light in life and love.

OLD LOVE SONG

Dreaming of love and romance throughout the

evening day,

and listening to old love songs and keeping them on
replay.

Makes you love and miss old moments in your life,

when you sit and really realize just how much time has
gone by.

KEY TO MY HEART

(Him)

My love, my love,

you are so beautiful to me.

Representing true beauty and the purity of a dove set
free.

I love you much,

and yet so much more.

Your beauty yet,

I so dearly adore.

You took my life as yet by siege,

holding my heart forever in captivity.

But only you my love,

holds the key.

KEY TO MY HEART

(Her)

My love, my love.

I asked, "Where art thou?"

Hidden away in this world's secrets here and now.

My heart cries out for thee undeniably so,

as my body yearns to be so very close.

I hope to soon find you wherever you may be,

because my heart still holds onto all

the love

and promises you made to me.

PAINTED SUNSETS

My love,

your lips are so sensual and yet so sweet.

Glistening with the dew and the precious nectar of life.

With remembrance of how I met you,

I gazed into your soulful eyes.

This I will remember and yet I will never forget,

because to me your love is as beautiful as

God's painted sunsets.

LOVE SONG

Your heart was as beautiful as the golden morning's sun,

for always when I am with you my heart has always sung.

Where laughter and joy always seem to follow us along.

This I can confess is our beautiful,

yet never forgotten

love song.

EMBRACING LOVE

As I stare at the chandelier's diamonds that are shining
their glistening light.
I tend to think inwardly to myself,

this is a lovely night.

Where much laughter and joy abound,

my heart rejoices at the very pleasant sound.

Knowing that tonight was the night I would see you,

standing by the pews.

You instantly embraced me with your loving arms,

because you knew I had missed you.

FATED LOVE

The peonies and the roses will soon be in bloom,
nearby the gardens gates.

My love for you is like that of rare beauty,

because I can't escape.

You trapped my heart in a blissful love,

leading to my forever fate.

Always wanting more of you,

but I fear I will be too late.

I hope that one day we will exchange our love and
thence seal our fate.

But I do know that loving you,

would never be a grave mistake.

LOVE

She always wanted a love that could pass the test of
time,
a love that encompassed both the bodies and the minds.

A love that could last the ages,

not just the current time.

A love that could write the pages of a love story upon
her beating heart.

She always wanted a love that could never be swayed or
sadly torn apart.

PEACHES AND CREAM

Your body is like that of a ripened peach,
as firm and beautiful as your lips are sweet.

Your lips are soft and taste like cream,

as your heart is warm and full of dreams.

My heart melts with love,

in your endearing embrace.

As I looked forward to sharing so many

love shared days.

TIMELESS LOVE

From Venice to France to the terrains of life,
my love for you will always stand the test of time.

For you,

stole my heart like a bandit hidden in the night.

This love is so beautiful,

I refused to fight.

I let you take me at your loving will,

for I knew I loved you and my heart was still.

You kissed me dearly in the sleepless nights,

as I embraced you with the love that comes with life.

MY DOVE

His body is like that of silk within his empire,

While my heart's emotions are always burning with desire.

I drink from his cup,

always wanting more.

My thirst cannot be quenched for him,

for he is so dearly adored.

Like a cool glass of milk,

I sip from his cup.

With every word that he speaks,

I can never get enough.

I feel overwhelmingly weak at the sight of my love,

for my heart always beats for him.

My darling,

my dove.

ALWAYS

We had a love,

so pure and joyful.

Bodies and souls facing heaven,

rejoiceful.

For it will forever be you and I.

I will love you always,

until the end of time.

Kiss of Eternity

A kiss in eternity and a tear in the eye,

as I gazed into your soulful memorizing eyes.

A kiss is warmed with the infinity of love,

a precious gift from the God of heaven above.

As I gazed upon your sleek brown hair,

I felt our souls merge together with care.

Our love melts together into a loving kiss,

as I gazed into your soulful eyes.

Eternity ties.

FOREVER

Forever we will share this love and be tied as one,

knowing in my heart that you were always the one.

Your lips are full of passion,

like a kiss to my soul.

Forever in my heart you'll always be there to console.

You transcend into my heart until the end of time,

knowing that my love for you will never diminish in time.

THE ONE

You are the one,

my love,

my guide.

An oath I bequeath to you,

my love,

my life.

A devoted lover of mine,

so pure,

so kind.

Forever will you hold my heart,

my companion, my friend.

Forever in my soul,

our love has no end.

LOVE IN LIFE

Where would we be without love?

Empty?

Not Whole?

Always in search of the light of life?

The love in life?

Love is so powerful on its own.

A song of love can provide healing words and the reassurance of love.

Where would we be without love?

Love is at the center of everything and the driving force of happiness.

Love is the very being of our very essence.

LOVE OF NIGHT

I love the night and all that it entails.

Being with you in the candlelight,

beautiful fairy tales.

The stories of love and romance,

that echoed through the night.

As we wish upon a star in the

night's forbidden light.

His Sunrays

His love is like the sun's rays in early May,

he warms my soul like the earth's moistened clay.

His smile is like the river that runs so wild and free,

his love has so dearly

captivated me.

His eyes are like mirrors,

that glistens and shine.

Knowing his love is as great and as dear as mine.

LUST OF LOVE

The lust of love of a woman's heart,

you will awaken if you so please.

For if you glance at her with lust in your soul,

and your eyes happen to meet.

You will awaken the love in a woman's heart,

you so dearly want to meet.

Not really knowing that it's love in her heart,

that she so dearly wants to keep.

For she only lusts for true love,

a love that she can always keep.

A love that embraces her soul,

and never makes her weep.

My Desire

My mind tends to drift and daydream of romance and love all
day long
It's beautiful and filled with thoughts of you,
as I hear the nightingale's beautiful song.

This love I cannot control or own in any way,
but I know this love is true for the beautiful words that
you say.

You dance through my thoughts and my emotions all day
long.

Even if I close my eyes,
I dream of you all night long.

I wake up every day with the taste of you on my lips,
always wanting more of you.
Yes, this is something I cannot resist.

You are my desire that fills my mind with lustful dreams
and fills my heart with hope.

A Summer's Love

The summer is so long,

and I am endeared with thoughts of you.

For summer is always fun,

when I am right beside you.

In the summer's night flair,

it's only me and you.

Always in search of the summer night's

romantic rendezvous.

LIFE'S ESSENCE

SUMMER'S BLISS

The day lilies and their yellow blossom blooms,
called all the hummingbirds with their sweet perfume.

The aroma of their sweetness and beauty fills all the
spring days,

you could imagine how I wish spring would so
desperately stay.

The hummingbirds are always humming with delight and
bliss,

I know spring too they would surely miss.

Then spring soon fades into a summery bliss,

then you'll receive summer's sweetness you won't want
to miss.

Spring's Joyous Songs

The roses and the lilies always sleep all winter long,
resting their beauty before spring sings its joyous songs.

While the cardinals and the blue jays never tend to
migrate south,

they always tend to wait old man winter out.

As winter passes and the snow soon turns to rain,

we always tend to get saddened by April's rainy days.

But those clouds will soon pass,

as they never seem to last too long.

Then we will get to enjoy all of springs joyous songs.

For the flowers will be in bloom to brighten up your day,

and all the beautiful spring creatures will soon be out to
play.

THE SECRET OF TIME

As the forest is scenic and full of life,
so are the rivers that run with time.

From the forest's warm, earthy floors,

that is watered with the gift of life we so dearly adore.

To the trees lying on the forest ground,

with the gradual passing of time that can no longer be
found.

These things are so simple,

yet so renowned.

We find ourselves standing in the present,

always wondering how.

FALLING LEAVES

As I walk outside on a cool autumn day,

I feel the wind blow through its seasons of change.

The leaves fall so hopelessly light,

being carried away in the midst of this beautiful life.

As time passes,

they will soon all fall.

Dancing through the air like a masquerade ball.

Gleaming with colors they shine so bright,

they glistened and they gleamed as they danced through
the night.

PETALS OF PERFUME

The petals of a flower are so strategically aligned,

they never worry about the passing of time.

They slowly bloom in the full essence of the spring day's
sun,

bringing about a bounty of beautiful perfumic aroma
wherever they are hung.

Climbing up to the skies to reach the summer's warming
rays,

we tend to only understand their beauty as we
hopelessly gaze.

SNOWFLAKES OF FATE

As I peered out the window and watched the snowy
flakes slowly fall,

I watched them build up on the land and create a cooled
blanket wall.

Being so peaceful,

yet shimmering in the nights frosty air.

The patterns that were weaved into the snowy flakes,
were woven with such care.

Each one is unique with its own special pattern,

reminded me that life never seemed so random.

CASCADING WATERS

The birds fly so effortlessly in the woven blue net sky.

As the trees and vegetation spring up quickly from the
waters of the riverbanks,
that are so full of life.

Days and weeks slowly pass by,
just as the waters cascade through the perception of
time.

Slowly flowing and not ever truly knowing which way to go,
the waters of the riverbanks always make their path
undeniably known.

Slowly cutting and carving the land,
even the waters know you cannot reverse your past.

Emersed in your emotions,
undeniably so.

All you can do is release them and let them flow.

THE APPLE BLOSSOMS

As the apple blossoms bloom with their appealing
fragrance and allure,

the honey-blossom bees began to take flight and stir.

Always in search of the sweetness and nectar of life,

and always humming with the melodies and the
precision of time.

As the apple blossoms bloom in full essence waiting to
be seen.

The honey blossom bees will soon begin their stay,

gathering all the pollen till summer slowly

fades away.

THE SEED OF TRUTH

The roses with their alluring aroma slowly climb up the
garden's gates,

twirling and twisting their vines as if this was their
destined fate.

Reaching for the sky and the sun's warming rays,

so they could delicately bloom and you could hopelessly
gaze.

Knowing that their beauty is untouched by man,

and understanding the seed of truth that all miracles are
by God's hands.

THE SPARROW'S SONG

The sparrows fly by on the brisk morning of a summer's
day,

always chirping and singing with their beautiful praise.

Dancing and at play in the garden's trails,

living their life as if it were a

beautiful fairy tale.

WINTER NIGHTS

As the crisp,

cool snow falls from the darkened night sky,

we tend to hear the coyotes lonesome howling cries.

With the full moon projecting its lovely lantern light,

you can hear the nocturnal birds soon begin taking flight.

Wisping their feathered wings through the

chilled night's air,

and resting their somber bodies when a branch is soon
near.

Waiting for the sun to begin to rise,

to give warmth to these beautiful yet cold winter nights.

EVENING SUNSET

The multitudes of colors shine out from the sky,

as I sit and watch the sun set in the beautiful evening
sky.

From precious pinks to a lace-covered orange hue,

the evening is brilliantly pieced together.

As I sit,

and the wind blew.

Knowing that everything is planned and pieced together

with such deliberate care,

and always appreciating how the world is so

beautifully fare.

PINK PEONIES

The peonies with their pink blossom blooms,

dance through spring as they continuously bloom.

As their petals fall and blanket the ground,

a beauty that can be compared cannot be found.

SPRING TO SUMMER

For when the snow melts and winter is gone,
the March lilies will soon spring up and sing their lovely
songs.
For spring will soon be here and the sparrows will then
take flight,
getting their nest ready for the warm summer nights.
Spring only lasts a short little while,
so enjoy the March lilies and don't forget to smile.
Their fragrant yellow blooms will soon begin to fade,
giving new room for the peonies to bloom and play.
Once they are gone their pink petals will cover the
ground,
then there will soon be roses in their place to be found.
Climbing up the lattice until the midst of the
summer's days.
Don't forget to enjoy their beauty,
for summer too will soon fade

LIGHTNING

A flash of lightning.
The God of Glory thunders.

Eternal crashing.

Lights streak across the sky.

A storm is rolling in.

You hear the crash of lightning.

What a light show!

SUNRISE

The ocean waves crash upon the shore,

the sun rises in the east as it has always done before.

The seagulls fly by as the sky slowly brightens,

the sunrise is adorned with beautiful shades of orange
and pastel pinks.

A FULL MOON

A full moon.

A night sky full of stars.

A moon as vivid as the sun.

You can hear the wolf's howl in the distance.

The phrase

"Night Life,"

shows its true meaning.

People gather as the moon shines brightly in the
darkened night sky.

To celebrate life, love, and the beauty of night,

in all its delight.

DAISIES

Daisies are pretty with their white-colored blossoms,

daffodils have style with their yellow blossom trumpets.

Spring is so beautiful and yet so sweet,

while all the March lilies have awoken from their sleep.

While all the daisies are painted with the whiteness and purity of love.

Dazzling in their beauty,

while God smiles above.

FLOWERS

Orchids are purple and white,

just as roses are painted red.

As I look across the field,

I can see the magnolias drenched in love.

In all their array of beauty sent from the God above.

They remind me of a dream of passion and love,

spreading their leaves and blossoms up to the morning
sun.

The sunflowers reach up to the light blue skies.

A blush of hazel, and so are your eyes.

Foxgloves in the hedges surround the garden gates.

My love for you,

I can no longer escape.

FOLLOW ME

The land.

The ocean.

In this world I travel.

The soul and beauty in my mind,

I swallow.

Those are my words for you to follow.

Follow me.

THE SEA

The Atlantic shore however hard it tries to stay calm,

will always be reckless.

It glistens in the sun on its peaceful days,

as it rages in the night with its crashing waves.

I cannot help but stop and gaze at its beauty.

Down, down, down,

into the darkness of its depths.

I often wonder how many secrets it has kept.

I watch as the waves crash upon the ocean shore.

I can smell the salt water in the crisp air,

where the waves are born.

Above all others is the Atlantic shore.

Untold Truths

THE OLD TIMERS TALE

As she listened to the stories the old-timers told,

she would start to see their lives begin to unfold.

They would tell her stories or even old truths,
back in the day when they lived in their youth.

Stories of love, stories of pain, stories of truth,
and that they felt they had lived in vain.

Wishing they knew back then what they know now,
they would have relived their lives somehow.

From what I believe they were trying to say is,

"I hope you don't regret your life someday."

Life is short and this is true,

and eventually one day you'll be telling your story too.

PERSPECTIVE ON LIFE

Always have an optimistic attitude even if you're feeling down,

because of our life's emotions they always follow us all around.

They follow us every morning,

until the time we lay down.

If you think of grief all day long,

you'll soon begin to frown.

Grief will bring you heartache and you'll sing a saddened song.

Whereas if you focus more on joy,

all your troubles will seem gone.

LIVING LIFE

For she always lived her life full of joy and bliss.

Knowing that life would soon pass her by,

and that there was not a moment she would miss.

For she always saw others in life who would only hope
and wish,

Knowing this was the one message they had clearly
missed.

While others only dreamed of the life they could've had,

she was always busy living the life they wished they had.

For never let life pass you by,

for our time here is short before we say,

"Goodbye."

A Helping Heart

For her life was never perfect and she always had ups
and downs,
but she never let this affect her because she always
refused to frown.

For her,

life was more than the emotions she had always felt.

For she knew that in this life,

everybody needed someone's help.

For she always tried to smile and lend a helping hand,

knowing all the while not everyone in this world

would truly understand.

THE BOASTER

Men love to boast and speak of great things,

but what is there to truly be gained?

An inflated ego?

A false sense of self?

False friends that are never there for you,

when you need their help?

A woman who only cares for the things that you say,
but when she finds out the truth will her love be
swayed?

If her love was for herself and not yet for you,
you may have swayed her with your words and invited
yourself to be used.

So pay attention to the words that you speak,
and remember that being humble doesn't mean that
you are weak.

GOLDEN HEART

What is beauty?

An alluring presence?

Or is beauty a soul-found essence?

Within a heart you'll find true love,

but most seek the beauty that lies above.

Like a golden heart with a lock and a key,

this seems to represent true beauty to me.

A KIND WORD

Live your life in the sweetest of ways,

being nice and taking the time to listen to what people

say.

For a lot of people are hurting,

and you never know to what extent.

Until you take the time to speak with them,

and learn your words could've been a gift.

A BEAUTIFUL GIFT

Being a free spirit Is not understanding the worldly

ways,

just as she danced in the night's mesmerizing rains.

As people told her not to,

as this was not their way.

She was reluctant,

and her free spirit could not be swayed.

For she felt that life was free to live,

and that love was a gift.

So why not live your life as a

precious beautiful gift?

A WOMAN'S HEART

A woman always craves a man's love no matter her age.

Not a physical desire,

but a love that comes with grace.

For if a woman is alone her heart will be

saddened,

because she lacks the love of a devoted

companion.

THOUGHTS ON AGING

Never wanting to grow old and never wanting to
age,
will leave you in a deposition of never acquiring
much grace.

For all men and women will soon go down this
path,
aging is a milestone don't regret your past.

But as we age,
we will soon lose our youth.
But it was given in exchange to acquire much
truth.

PASSING OF TIME

For time seems to pass through an hourglass,

like sand passing through our fingertips.

We never gain a true grip because it passes so fast.

Every second is a gift,

so choose wisely how you live.

Because most of the time we are unaware of our actions

and how we truly live.

THE HEART & MIND

What are emotions other than our heartfelt thoughts

brought out to play?

Leaving no room for intellectual thinking,

because we choose to listen to what they say.

For a heart can be pure in the most beautiful of ways,

but without intellectual thinking you may end up getting

played.

For not everyone's intent is always pure and good,

some people have motives and are up to no good.

.

A Hurtful Heart

Some people like to hurt people intentionally so,

some will even take the initiative and take a low blow.

Some people like to hurt others because this is their will,

Only to cause you pain, suffering, and ill will.

Sometimes it's from rivalry and sometimes it's not.

Sometimes it's from jealousy,

because they wish they had what you got.

The only way to fix this is to truly let it go,

because the more you're in their presence the more

their jealousy and rivalry will grow.

For the problem does not lie with you,

even though this is what they try to make you believe.

The problem lies with them,

because their hearts are full of envy and greed.

SAD REALIZATION

When you keep trying to help someone and
keep giving them what you have,
sometimes you need to take a step backwards
and start adding up the math.
For if they always take from you,
and they feel as if it weren't enough.
Maybe it's because they never respected you,
even though you're doing it out of
love.

NEVER ALONE

A sad and lonely heart is never something to dismiss,

sometimes all it takes is a hug and a happy kiss to fix

this.

Sometimes a heart can be broken and never quite the

same,

this is usually when someone has gone through

so much

heart-wrenching pain.

Even though they smile and tell you everything's okay,

always remember to be there for them when they are

not acting quite the same.

For the love and generosity that you show them,

you can cure so much pain.

Just by letting them know you're there for them,

and that everything will be okay.

AWAKENING

Her heart was bent and broken,

and she never understood all the words that he had

spoken.

He spoke of love and the endearments of life,

but all he ever did was bring strife into her life.

For his words were false,

but her heart was true.

This is a warning,

do not let this happen to you.

A GOOD WILL

To stand in the knowledge of truths and virtues,

you realize that being a good person in the end may

hurt you.

You choose to help others in the midst of this,

because you realize loving others is our biggest gift.

By loving others you will lend a helping hand.

But if you lack a heart,

this you will never understand.

THE SANDS OF TIME

I want to live a life in love with no rain,

I want to live a life full of desire and no pain.

Live a life rich in joy and not in vain,

live life with you in my hands.

Not live a life like the sands of time,

with you passing through my hands.

SORROW

Sorrow is from sorrow,

this is sometimes a hard truth to swallow.

Sorrow and grief go hand in hand,

in the land of tears and sadness.

We then grow weary of our lack of hope and gladness,

we are always sorry for our sorrow and grief.

Perhaps we will grow stronger and soon get relief.

HAPPINESS

Happiness is sometimes just a word,

time flies by totally unheard.

Happiness is our choice,

our decision at hand.

For will you be happy?

or

Will you be sad?

We cannot depend on another individual to change our
feelings or our minds,

for sometimes this lesson is never learned in time.

GROWING PAINS

Oh,

it has been such a year of growing pains,

oh my, oh dear.

This world has dealt with such tragedy,

from a pandemic to the beginning of WWIII.

Not everything can always remain the

same you see,

but this world is better without all the tragedies and all
the pain.

THE LOVE OF JESUS

My life is not a tale of love and joy.

It was dark and cold.

No happiness.

No Joy.

What I did just to be seen.

A heart without love is lifeless,

it seems.

The pain you feel when your mind is not free.

But with the love of Jesus Christ,

I know I can start over all clean.

THE LIGHT

The sun shines its rays on those who live for the light.

The angels in heaven always sing and fight the good
fight.

They can feel the love of God's almighty might.

There is no room for darkness,

for those who live in the light.

For darkness will flee at the calling of his name,

all you must do is praise his holy name.

A Viking's Tale

An old Viking saying or even an old truth.

Is when the shadows rise and the sorrows creep near,

stand fast and steady and refuse to fear!

Sharp in your mind and strong in your body,

sharpen your sword and always stand ready!

THE COZY HOME

Whose house is that?

I think I know.

Its owner is quite happy, though.

Full of joy like a vivid rainbow.

I watch him laugh,

I cry hello.

The home is gray, cozy, and deep,

the owner has many promises to keep.

In the morning,

he rises from his bed to think about the long day ahead.

HEARTBREAKING MOMENTS

FREEDOM

When you're broken and don't feel like you can go on
in life.
You always tend to blame others for the misery in your
life,
which always leads to tears falling from your eyes.

You're always left wondering,
why is there so much strife stirred up in your life?

If you take the time to heal,
then you would clearly see.
There are so many beautiful things in this life
that could truly set you free.

THE MAN WITH THE MASK

For her heart was broken and she could not express herself,

she couldn't even get closure to try to help herself.

He refused to speak and tell her what was wrong.

But in her mind,

she characterized him as if he couldn't do anything wrong.

For all she could see was what she wanted to believe,

she chose to believe in all the illusions she had built him up to

be.

For he wore a false mask and hid who he really was.

But this was how he used women,

by making them believe he was their one true love.

Some time passed and she still couldn't understand,

how can a man touch me and not love me for who I am?

Until enough time passes,

and she strips away his mask.

Only then will she realize he does this to all women,

and would no longer be sad.

JACK

The days are long since you have been gone,

I wish I could have forever held you in my loving arms.

You were my little boy,

so dear and sweet.

My little Jack Russell doggy,

I wish you didn't have to leave.

You made my heart whole every day that you were here,

but when you departed you left my heart broken into tears.

EMBROIDERED HEART

She wore flowers that embroidered her heart,

never expecting him to pick them apart.

They were delicate and beautiful,

like that of a precious dove.

Each petal represented a token of her unfailing love.

HURTFUL WORDS

Some people say things that they know aren't true,

just to tear you apart emotionally and to try to get to you.

They spew venom from their lips in hopes of breaking your heart.

Knowing they caused you pain and suffering,

and to watch you fall apart.

LOSING HOPE

You blame everyone else but never yourself for all the
things wrong in your life,

but you never consider your circumstances
may have come from you choosing how to live your life.

You chose your actions whether they were good or bad,

then laid all the blame and all the resentment on all the
friends that you had.

When no one's left,

because you ran them all away.

Will you eventually learn it was from your own sour
attitude in life,

that drove them all away?

IN TOO DEEP

When you're in too deep,

sometimes you feel like you're in a hole.

So deep and dark,

that you felt like you've lost all control.

When you're in too deep it can feel like an uphill battle.

In the moments that seem grim,

it can feel like a hopeless battle.

LOVE IS DEAD

Love can feel like dread,

when your soul is so full of pain and dread.

My eyes are blood red.

No sleep.

No bed.

Who can awaken love?

When a man shatters your heart,

rips it into pieces and tears it apart?

When I look into the past,

I see the monster he became.

With his lack of love,

and his intentions to play me as a game.

THERE IS STILL HOPE

The heavy heart is a plague of hopelessness that eats
away at your soul.

When you feel as though he has abandoned you,

you become lost in the midst of your pain.

Only hoping and wishing that the love could've
somehow been sustained.

As the nights seem lonely and dark,

the heartache engulfs your being.

You soon begin to realize that this darkness fades with
time,

and that there is still hope for you.

If you give yourself enough time.

LOVE IS GONE

It was good and pleasant from the start,

I never expected him to tear my heart apart.

From the beginning,

I thought you were a man.

A man of morals, respect, and virtues,

a true gentleman.

Never judge a book by its cover.

For the love is gone for now,

but not forever.

I'm in Heaven

I hope you look at the sky and smile like I do.

Now that I'm gone,

I chase a rainbow or two.

Until I fall asleep with the colors that I meet.

If only you could see the colors of red and pastel pinks.

I made it to heaven,

I'll be on the other side waiting for you.

Always remember to love your life.

I WISH

I wish I was yours,

like the waves have the shores.

I wish I could make you smile every day,

not just once in a while.

You're the best feeling within,

your kiss is love, desire, and bliss.

My heart has always been yours from the start,

but it's a little broken and falling apart.

Is True Love A Lie?

True love?

You told me you would always love me.

Was there no truth?

Perhaps our love was a wish,

unfulfilled and ungranted in our youth.

Maybe you never believed,

I am forced to bid you farewell.

UNLOVED

I could never have loved anyone the way I loved you,

I would have followed you throughout time.

Our passion was a vow and an endearing promise of love between us.

It cuts me more than you will ever know,

may we both find happiness and peace.

REMEMBER ME

Don't remember me the way I am,
remember me the way I was.

Everything I wanted to do,

and everything I dreamed of doing.

DEDICATION

This book is dedicated to all our family, friends, and

everyone we hold dear to our hearts.

But mostly this book is dedicated to our

Lord and Savior,

Jesus Christ.

ABOUT THE AUTHORS

Linda Diane Lay, Angelia Richhart, and Amber Richhart are poets, writers, and authors of multiple great books. They reside in Indiana and have a love for poetry and the arts. They have written an inspirational book named "Divinely Guided," which surrounds and entails the subjects of faith, love, hope, peace, and joy. While this book offers an inspirational message of love and acceptance through Jesus Christ, this book is based on Christianity and love. It is a good read for anyone wanting to learn more about Christianity, deepen their faith, and strengthen their relationship with Jesus Christ.

They have also written three poetic books that are anthologies, which are collections of poems from each author compiled together in one beautiful work, such as "The Sugar Orchard," "Poetic Colors," and "The Essence of a Pearl." These books dive deep into the depths of femininity and the emotions that women feel throughout life. Such as love, joy, and bliss, as well as exploring the sad poetic symphonies of pain, grief, and loss, while offering beautifully hand-drawn images to separate each unique chapter. These books have words that will touch your heart and soul, as well as words of wisdom, heartache, love, and grief that we have all felt throughout our lives. The words they use reflect such deep emotions that you will have cried the tears they have shed, shared the joy and feel as if you have encountered these life experiences yourself.

Linda Diane Lay, Angelia Richhart, and Amber Richhart use such passion and poetic expression when they write that the pages are engulfed in raw emotions. Anyone who reads their words from any of their poetic books can always relate to the emotions that they have felt.